TAKE A PICTURE

By
SUSAN CHAMPAGNE

SAMUEL FRENCH, INC.
45 West 25th Street   NEW YORK 10010
7623 Sunset Boulevard HOLLYWOOD 90046
LONDON   TORONTO

Copyright ©, 1989, by Susan Champagne

ALL RIGHTS RESERVED

CAUTION: Professionals and amateurs are hereby warned that TAKE A PICTURE is subject to a royalty. It is fully protected under the copyright laws of the United States of America, the British Commonwealth, including Canada, and all other countries of the Copyright Union. All rights, including professional, amateur, motion pictures, recitation, lecturing, public reading, radio broadcasting, television, and the rights of translation into foreign languages are strictly reserved. In its present form the play is dedicated to the reading public only.

TAKE A PICTURE may be given stage presentation by amateurs in theatres seating less than 500 upon payment of a royalty of Fifty Dollars for the first performance, and Twenty-five Dollars for each additional performance. PLEASE NOTE: for amateur productions in theatres seating over 500, write for special royalty quotation, giving details as to ticket price, number of performances and exact number of seats in your theatre. Royalties are payable one week before the opening performance of the play, to Samuel French, Inc., at 45 W. 25th St., New York, NY 10010; or at 7623 Sunset Blvd., Hollywood, CA 90046, or to Samuel French (Canada), Ltd., 80 Richmond St. East, Toronto, Ontario, Canada M5C 1P1.

Royalty of the required amount must be paid whether the play is presented for charity or gain and whether or not admission is charged.

Stock royalty quoted on application to Samuel French, Inc.

For all other rights than those stipulated above, apply to Samuel French, Inc.

Particular emphasis is laid on the question of amateur or professional readings, permission and terms for which must be secured in writing from Samuel French, Inc.

Copying from this book in whole or in part is strictly forbidden by law, and the right of performance is not transferable.

Whenever the play is produced the following notice must appear on all programs, printing and advertising for the play: "Produced by special arrangement with Samuel French, Inc."

Due authorship credit must be given on all programs, printing and advertising for the play.

Anyone presenting the play shall not commit or authorize any act or omission by which the copyright of the play or the right to copyright same may be impaired.

No changes shall be made in the play for the purpose of your production unless authorized in writing.

The publication of this play does not imply that it is necessarily available for performance by amateurs or professionals. Amateurs and professionals considering a production are strongly advised in their own interests to apply to Samuel French, Inc., for consent before starting rehearsals, advertising, or booking a theatre or hall.

No part of this book may be reproduced, stored in a retrieval system, or transmitted in any form, by any means, including mechanical, electronic, photocopying, recording, or otherwise, without the prior written permission of the publisher.

ISBN 0 573 69083 9   Printed in U.S.A.

IMPORTANT BILLING AND CREDIT REQUIREMENTS

All producers of TAKE A PICTURE *must* give credit to the Author of the Play in all programs distributed in connection with performances of the Play and in all instances in which the title of the Play appears for purposes of advertising, publicizing or otherwise exploiting the Play and/or a production. The name of the Author *must* also appear on a separate line, in which no other name appears, immediately following the title, and *must* appear in size of type not less than fifty percent the size of the title type.

TAKE A PICTURE was produced at the Padua Hills Playwrights' Festival in July, 1987. The play was also presented in October, 1987, at THE BOYD STREET THEATRE, Los Angeles, with the following cast:

CHARLES	Lee Kissman
LILY	Molly Cleator
RICHARD	Gregory Pace
CICI	Roxanne Rogers

Directed by Susan Champagne
Produced by Jay Green and Pipeline Productions
Set Design by Molly Cleator
Lighting Design by Cecile Galluzo
Stage Managers, Luis Alfaro, Cathy Comenas, Tobi Redlich

CHARACTERS

CHARLES

LILY

RICHARD

CICI

FOR LEE

TAKE A PICTURE

SETTING: Ensenada, Mexico. The play takes place is several bars, two motel rooms, a church, and a restaurant. The set should be very minimal. A full-size bed, two chairs, and a dressing screen on one side of the stage should define Motel Room. Two tables and four chairs on the other side of the stage should define Restaurant or Bar. The two transition scenes between LILY and CHARLES take place in the bar and on the dance floor (which is part of the bar.)

SCENE: As the audience is almost totally settled in, a slow Mexican WALTZ plays, introducing us to our setting: a motel room that is cheap and simple, very colorful, perhaps with pictures or decor that remind us of a 50s Americanized concept of a romantic Mexico. After the music has played for about two minutes, LIGHTS fade. After several seconds, the LIGHTS slowly come up. We now see LILY and CHARLES. They stand on opposite ends in front of the foot of a double bed, their backs to each other. They are totally still for several seconds. LILY wears glasses, a shirt buttoned up to the neck, an old-fashioned button-up sweater, a skirt, and sensible "walking shoes." She carries a goofy suitcae. CHARLES wears glasses, a white shirt, tie, old-fashioned dress slacks, and old-fashioned shoes. He carries a jug of water and a green suit coat and suitcase—both of which were once very nice. Now they are old and somewhat weathered. Shortly after the lights are up full, LILY turns toward CHARLES, MUSIC fades, and the play begins—

LILY. Well, here we are! EnsenAda, Mexico! *(She mispronounces EnsenAda.)*

CHARLES. *(He corrects her—)* Ensenada.

LILY. Ensenada. The Flamingo Motel!

CHARLES. The Flamingo Motel. Is it O.K.?

LILY. Yeah ... Oh. There's only one bed.

CHARLES. Is that O.K.?

LILY. *(insecure smile)* Sure.

CHARLES. I'm so tired. Maybe you should try it out.

LILY. O.K. *(LILY sits on bed.)*

CHARLES. Is it soft enough? *(He sits next to her on bed.)*

LILY. It's soft. *(They are both sitting on the bed. She nervously smiles, stands up and looks out "window.")*

LILY. It's a nice room. Very "colorful." Oh, look at the view. What is that tree?

CHARLES. Banana.

LILY. Oh, a banana tree! Wow! I wonder if it has bananas on it. In Connecticut they don't grown bananas. Probably because it's not a tropical climate. *(Smiles. CHARLES takes a tequila bottle out of his coat pocket, takes a drink.)*

CHARLES. Do you want some?

LILY. Me? No. Well — O.K. *(She takes some and coughs a lot. He pats her on the back until she stops coughing. Then he puts a jug of water to her mouth. She drinks water—)* Thank you.

CHARLES. This is as good a place as any.

LILY. Sure. It's a nice "colorful" place.

CHARLES. The other places, all they have is fancier rooms. Maybe a dining room—

LILY. If the Flamingo had a dining room, it's probably

be closed for Christmas and Christmas Eve. You made a good choice, Charles.

CHARLES. Cheaper.

LILY. Cheaper. So we can save money. I'm glad you met my Aunt Ethel in that bar. That's why I'm here! That's why we're roommates!

CHARLES. It's only been ten days—

LILY. Yeah, but — *(She smiles at him and shyly looks away as smile fades. He looks at her. She catches him looking at her. They both shyly look away. Pause.)* I think I'll find work soon. I really do. You know I used to be a cashier at the movies. The Pussycat Theatre is right up the block from the apartment.

CHARLES. *(Laughs.)* No.

LILY. Ha?

CHARLES. It's not the right kind of place.

LILY. Ha?

CHARLES. Adult movies.

LILY. Adult movies? Well I'm an adult. *(pause)* Oh. *(He stretches his arms and goes from a sitting position to lying on the bed. She sees this and stands up—)* I'm glad I'm not in Connecticut now. It's Christmas and I'm warm. And there's no money in electrology back there. People don't mind being hairy back there. In Los Angeles, places like that. people hate hair. Because they want to be in the movies. They hate having mustashes because for a woman it doesn't look good on the cameras. We learnt about the most vain people in electrology school. Probably because the most vain people are our best customers. *(She smiles at him. He is now near her. She had been saying most of the previous "monologue" while looking out "window" so—)*

CHARLES. Why do you talk so much?

LILY. Oh. I'm sorry. *(He puts his hand to her mouth gently—)*

CHARLES. Don't be. *(pause)* Maybe we should unpack. *(They do.)* You've never been to a foreign country?

LILY. I've never been out of Connecticut.

CHARLES. Los Angeles is very different than Connecticut, ha? Look what I got us for later. *(—a joint from his suitcase)*

LILY. Oh. Is that "grass?"

CHARLES. Ah ha.

LILY. Is it O.K. having illegal drugs in a foreign country? I'd hate to go to jail.

CHARLES. Yeah, it's pretty bad in the jail down here.

LILY. How do you know?

CHARLES. I was in it.

LILY. You were?

CHARLES. It's an old white building. Did you see "Midnight Express?"

LILY. Yeah.

CHARLES. Kinda like that.

LILY. How did it happen?

CHARLES. I don't know. They just got me. 'Cause I was walking around on the street. Singing. By myself. Drunk.

LILY. Oh. by yourself? *(He nods.)* You must have been upset.

CHARLES. I was. *(He sits.)*

LILY. What happened? *(She sits.)*

CHARLES. Oh. I don't know. I think my, you know, my, you know former *(pause)* wife I think that's when she left.

LILY. Oh. *(pause)* Why did she leave?

CHARLES. It's one of those complicated things with more than one reason.

LILY. Oh, sure.

CHARLES. It wasn't her fault, though.

LILY. No.

CHARLES. Wanna see a picture of her?

LILY. O.K. *(CHARLES takes out his wallet and shows LILY a photo—)* God, she looks like a movie star. This one, together, you both look like movie stars ... I don't get this one. Why are you both standing next to a giant ... heart?

CHARLES. Oh. That one. No, that's a liver. She was a nurse and I used to be a doctor.

LILY. Oh. *(pause)* You like what you're doing now, you know laying tile in bathrooms and kitchens, better than being a doctor? *(He shrugs and stares at the picture in his wallet that she had given back to him. She looks at him. He catches her looking at him. They both shyly look away. He puts his wallet away. She resumes unpacking. Shyly standing next to her suitcase on the bed, she puts things that were in the suitcase in a bag.)*

CHARLES. Why are you shoving those things in a bag?

LILY. These things?

CHARLES. Yeah. Let me see.

LILY. What?

CHARLES. What you're shoving in a bag like that ... *(He playfully tries to get the bag from her. He grabs it, smiles, and pulls out what she had in the bag, gives her the bag and looks away.)* My wife used to be like that. She'd hide all her underwear under my sweat socks. She wouldn't hang her underwear on the clothesline. Very, very shy. By the end, she didn't care. You wouldn't believe what you'd see out there on the line.

LILY. Really?

CHARLES. Ah ha. So I-I understand. *(pause)* Oh nice shoes.

LILY. You like 'em O.K.?

CHARLES. Yeah. They're kind of like shoes from the 30s.

LILY. My mother has a pair. *(She takes a wallet out of her purse—)* That's her and my father in the 30s. See them there on her feet?

CHARLES. She's kind of old now?

LILY. I'm a change of life baby same as my cousin Eloise. *(Smiles.)* These are OK for Midnight Mass?

CHARLES. Fine.

LILY. Can't really wear high heals because of the family foot condition.

CHARLES. What's wrong with the family feet?

LILY. Oh. I don't know. My mother's left foot bends this way so she walks like this *(Demonstrates.)* until she wears the corrective shoe and then *(Demonstrates.)* she walks like this. *(When she had done the corrective walk, she self-consciously stared at her feet in a funny way. He copies this, gently having fun with her—)*

CHARLES. Like this?

LILY. No. Kind of like this. *(She walks more normally.)*

CHARLES. Like this? *(He walks kind of normally.)*

LILY. Yeah. You got it. *(She sits on bed. He kneels near her feet—)*

CHARLES. Excuse me. Your foot?

LILY. My foot? Oh. Mine's OK now. *(He gestures, can he see it?)* O.K.

CHARLES. Oh. Let me snap your toes.

LILY. Excuse me?

CHARLES. It'll make you feel better.

LILY. Oh ... O.K. *(Pause, he begins snapping—)* It won't do anything weird to — to the FEEL of my toes ... *(She pulls her foot away from him. He stands up. She says, "I'm sorry." He touches his fingers to her mouth. He gets his coat.)* It was nice of you to offer — *(pause)* Are-are you a foot doctor?

CHARLES. No. *(pause)* It's just something I do well — You wanna go eat?

LILY. Sure. Nice coat.

CHARLES. Really?

LILY. It's a very pretty color.

CHARLES. I haven't worn this in a while.

LILY. Why?

CHARLES. It reminds me of — *(pause)* I don't wear green anymore.

LILY. That's from one of the pictures. *(He nods.)* You look very handsome.

CHARLES. No.

LILY. You really do.

CHARLES. Shall we? *(He offers his arm.)*

LILY. We shall. *(She takes his arm.)*

(Mexican MUSIC comes up as LILY and CHARLES got to the bar. As mentioned in the description of the setting, all transition scenes are like silent movies. The MUSIC is instrumental, quirky, humorous and, in a way, old-fashioned. In this scene, which lasts two to three minutes, LILY and CHARLES Enter the bar.

TAKE A PICTURE

CHARLES shows LILY how to drink tequila in Mexico: make a fist, put salt on the fist, lick the salt, drink the tequila, and suck on a lime. All this is mimed. LILY copies him. We can tell she doesn't like or isn't used to sucking salt and lime and drinking tequila, but she smiles at CHARLES after each move: she wants to like this new adventure. When the MUSIC changes, CHARLES asks LILY silently, "Wanna go smoke a joint?" She nods. He takes her hand and they walk to what we think might be an alley. He makes sure that no one is looking and he lights the imaginary joint and takes a hit of it. He shows her how to inhale. She copies him, but she coughs. A lot. She bends over because she's coughing so much. He slaps her back. After a bit, she smiles an "I'm OK" smile, but when he takes another hit, a stoned sick feeling takes over. We see this on her face. When he looks at her she smiles. He offers her the joint. She takes a hit and has another coughing spell. He pats her on the back. The MUSIC changes again. He asks her silently, "Do you wanna go eat?" She smiles. When she follows him, the pot is really taking it's toll. She looks at the back of her skirt and touches it as if her slip has bunched way up on her. When he looks at her, she smiles. This happens twice. He pulls her chair out for her when they are in the restaurant. She points to a painting and smiles. He looks at it too and smiles. He gestures to her imaginary plate. She nods and smiles. He eats his meal. She is too sick to eat hers and looks away from him with a sick look on her face. When he looks at her, she smiles at him and looks at her plate. This happens three times. The third time, he's upset because she's not eating and she keeps saying things are OK. He leaves the restaurant upset. She follows behind him, paranoid and occasionally looking at the back of her skirt for that slip she feels is riding up on her. They Enter motel room as MUSIC ends— —.)

CHARLES. All that money wasted and you didn't even eat — And all these people starving.

LILY. I told you that "grass," I never had it before and it makes me kind of goofy in the head.

CHARLES. Goofy in the head?

LILY. I can't, you know re-remember myself. I'll feel all better after a little nap. I promise you, Charles. *(She puts her head down on bed.)* I — I don't want the people to starve in the street. I really don't. I gave that little chicklet girl some of these paper dineris.

CHARLES. Dinero. That won't change anything.

LILY. Well she and the mother can eat something—

CHARLES. There will always be suffering in the world. You can't *cure* suffering. The people who *could* change things and the people you *want* to LISTEN—

LILY. What?

CHARLES. —Don't. *(pause)* Nothing.

LILY. You were talking kind of softly. *(He nods. She sits up.)* I listen to you — I *love* to listen to you. Really. I swear to God. *(He doesn't respond.)* Could-Could I have some more of that stuff you have? *(He gives her his tequila bottle. She takes a sip, starts to cough, but stops the cough and smiles at him. She gives him the bottle—)* You have some too. *(He does.)* You know, the chicken mole looked good. *(She mispronounces mole.)*

CHARLES. *(He laughs and pronounces the Spanish word—)* Molé.

LILY. Molé. *(Smiles.. They look at each other and smile. After a bit, they shyly look away.)*

CHARLES. Want me to snap your toes now?

LILY. Will it help?

CHARLES. Yeah.

LILY. O.K.

CHARLES. *(He begins massaging and snapping—)* Maybe your mother's foot problem has something to do with some other problem. Each part of the foot corresponds to a part of the body. That's why a good foot massage will relax your whole body—

LILY. *(pause)* What part of me are you trying to get to? *(Smiles. He is kneeling near her. She is sitting on the bed, her upper body bent over to her knees watching him. When she says this, she doesn't realize what she's just said. They look at each other after this line. His face moves toward her wanting to kiss her. There is a small moment where this kiss could happen, but she stands up. She is very nervous and she talks quickly while he stays in his kneeling position and occasionally looks at her. She can't look at him. And says the following while looking out the imaginary window, which is downstage—)* God, I wonder what part of my mother's body and what part of her, you know, foot, are related and maybe if she has another problem. I should call her when we get back and tell her about her feet. And, you know, what to do with a foot doctor or what the part is. I wonder what she's doing now. Christmas. I wonder what they're all doing now in bed. I mean no. I mean not what they're doing in bed. I don't want to know that. It's none of my business. What they're thinking of in their *sleep* Christmas Eve and what they could possibly be — *(CHARLES is standing near her now. He gently puts his hand to her mouth. She looks at him and becomes quiet.)*

CHARLES. Who are you talking to?

LILY. Oh. *(pause)* You?

CHARLES. Why can't you look at me when you speak?

(He smiles and gently holds her face with his hands, facing her toward him.)

LILY. Oh.

CHARLES. You're just saying things because you're scared.

LILY. NO I'M NOT. *(He looks at her and walks away. He grabs his coat and heads for the bar. She puts her sock and shoe back on and runs out after him. She waits in the bar for him. He comes back with two drinks. He doesn't really look at her, puts the drinks on the table. They both sit in silence. Finally—)* You know the chicken mole looked good. I just never thought of mixing chocolate and chili together. It's a good idea, though. You know, the two CHs. *(pause)* What's wrong? *(She gently puts her hand on his. He retrieves it and uses it to find a cigarette in his pocket. He lights the cigarette and smokes. He doesn't look at her. She looks at her drink. After a silence—)* I'm going to the bathroom.

(As she leaves for the bathroom, she bumps into RICHARD. RICHARD and CICI have just Entered. RICHARD stares at LILY even after she's left. CICI sees this and grabs his face and gives him a big dramatic kiss. They sit. CICI notices CHARLES. RICHARD sees this and gives her a big showy kiss. RICHARD takes his polaroid out and prepares to take a snap shot of CICI. He fluffs her hair out and she strikes a semi-exotic, semi-drunk pose. He snaps the picture. They both sit. They both look at CHARLES, look at each other and nod. RICHARD Exits. He returns with two drinks and puts them on CHARLES' and LILY'S table. CICI Exits. LILY Enters and sits back at the table.)

LILY. *(of their new drinks—)* What happened?

CHARLES. They ordered us drinks.// LILY. Who?
CHARLES. That couple over there.
LILY. *(Looks and smiles at them.)* How nice.
CHARLES. We should ask them to join us.

LILY. Sure. *(CICI and RICHARD are already there at the table. CICI'S brought over drinks for her and RICHARD. RICHARD'S brought down their own two chairs. CICI and RICHARD have obviously been partying and are probably pretty coked up. Their invasion on CHARLES and LILY is a very lively one. They speak quickly and are ready to party. They are dressed in "modern" club garb. CICI has on a nice amount of make-up and a sexy outfit. She also wears long red nails. They introduce themselves—)*

CICI. I'm Cici and this is my boyfriend, Richard.

CHARLES. Charles.

LILY. Lily.

CICI. Pleased to meet you. We were lookin' at you two over here and saying to ourselves, it's way too lonely for Americans to spend Christmas alone, right, honey? These two look like they care for a cocktail, I says. *(LILY says, "Thank you.")* Don't mention it. We're so happy to find you two. Look at everything else that's around here. That old drunk dancing back there and that really old thing who looks like Marlena Dietrich without a lift.

RICHARD. The prostitute?

CICI. Yeah. See her back there? Christmas Eve, you'd think she'd give it a rest. *(They all toast.)* Yeah, well as I was saying, it's a pleasure to find you two. *(They all shake hands. CICI takes LILY'S hand from RICHARD.)*

CICI. Oh. Such delicate little fingers. You should have

some work done.

LILY. Ha?

CICI. On your fingernails. I'm a manicurist.

LILY. Oh. Yeah. I really like yours. The color and they're so *long.*

CICI. It's easy, honey. Even with small fingernails like them.

RICHARD. They're synthetic.

LILY. What's that mean?

RICHARD. Synthetic. Fake. *(to CICI:)* You bite yours. You just tack those on. I know.

CICI. Pl—*EA*SE. *(pause)* Oh, you've got a spot on your glasses. Let me. *(She spits on LILY'S glasses to remove spot.)* I wouldn't charge you if you wanna come in. Just for supplies. You'd be a real before-and-after. I'd like to take pictures. *(She snaps a picture of LILY'S hand.(* Here's my card. We also have a facialist. She does mustaches, eyebrows, bikini wax. *(She looks LILY up and down.)* Do you ever wear a bikini?

LILY. No. *(Smiles.)* Never. I'm a registered electrologist. I don't need any hair removal. I've had it done already. During electrology school. *(Smiles.)*

CICI. *(Looks her up close.)* I guess so.

LILY. If you want me to do any work on you — *(Looks her up close.)*

CICI. No.

LILY. Here's my card. I just moved to Los Angeles ten days ago. And I don't have a practice yet and I don't work for anyone yet and I haven't even tried yet, but there's my card with my name and phone number written on it. *(Short pause — CICI stares at CHARLES. RICHARD stares at*

LILY. They suck their drinks down. When CICI finishes hers—)

CICI. All done. *(to RICHARD)* Honey — *(to LILY)* This is my little boy, Jacques—

RICHARD. *(to LILY:)* He's a chink. The father. The eyes there.

CICI. He's sixteen months now. I left him with my mother. It's his first Christmas, but he won't even remember it. Buy them more drinks.

RICHARD. *(to waiter:)* Hey — Hey — I said come over here. Jesus, these Mexicans!

CICI. You're Mexican, honey.

RICHARD. Half.

CICI. We might get married tomorrow. Nothing fancy. After breakfast. You can be our attendants.

RICHARD. O.K. I'm gonna take a picture.

CICI. It's nice. We turn 'em into slides and blow 'em up and then show 'em for people.

RICHARD. *(to LILY:)* What are you, about a 34B?

CICI. We have a house out on the beach. The plumbing's all messed up so that's why we're at El Cid. Where are you at again?

CHARLES. The Flamingo.

CICI. Oh. That's right.

RICHARD. *(to LILY and CHARLES:)* Get closer. Come on. Pretend that you like each other. *(LILY and CHARLES sit close to each other. RICHARD looks LILY up and down with his camera, finally takes the picture.)* Do you wanna dance?

LILY. O.K. *(They dance to a Mexican song, slow.)*

CICI. So what do you do for a living?

CHARLES. Tile.

CICI. Tile?

CHARLES. I lay tile.

CICI. That must pay well. *(He shrugs.)* Can I bum a cigarette?

CHARLES. Sure. *(He lights her cigarette. She looks at him and smiles. he smiles back. Pause.)*

CICI. You wanna dance, too?

CHARLES. Well—

CICI. No?

CHARLES. O.K. *(CHARLES and CICI, and LILY and RICHARD all dance to the slow dance. RICHARD thinks a group of men are all looking at CICI—)*

RICHARD. Hey, what're you lookin' at? This is my wife.

CICI. Honey. Honey, don't. They weren't lookin' like that at me. They were lookin' like that at her.

RICHARD. O.K. *(pause)* Why isn't he doin' something?

CICI. Ask him.

RICHARD. You see how they're looking at her? Why don't you do anything?

LILY. They're not looking at me, are they? *(to CHARLES:)*

RICHARD. They are. They're looking at you.

CICI. Honey—

RICHARD. Aren't you married?

CHARLES. No.

RICHARD. Well, you live together?

CHARLES. No.

RICHARD. I don't get it. Will you look? They're, they're lookin'—

CICI. Honey — *(to CHARLES:)* We're gonna have to switch. *(They do. CHARLES and LILY, RICHARD and CICI dance together.)* Honey, let's just close our eyes. Let's — *(They all dance. RICHARD and CICI slowly come to dance very closely almost melting into each other. CHARLES and LILY are shy and awkwardly keep a distance from each other. When the dance ends, they sit. Pause. They are quiet.)*

RICHARD. *(to LILY and CHARLES:)* What do you want, same? *(CHARLES nods.)* The service is so slow.

CICI. Honey, drink your cocktail.

RICHARD. Don't tell me what to do. *(pause)*

CICI. So what do the two of you do for a living?

CHARLES. Tile.

CICI. Oh, that's right. And you with the hair plucking.

LILY. Well it's not really plucking, it's—

CICI. *(to CHARLES:)* What do you do for fun? *(CHARLES shrugs.)*

RICHARD. What are you doing later tonight?

RICHARD and CICI. Do you like Coke?

LILY. We're going to Midnight Mass. *(CICI and RICHARD look at each other. RICHARD goes to the bar and cancels drinks.)*

RICHARD. We gotta be goin'.

CICI. Honey — *(She runs after him.)* We'll see you later — Why don't you stop by, 34B *(They Exit. A long awkward pause.)*

LILY. Cheers.

CHARLES. Cheers.

LILY. Where are our drinks?

CHARLES. I think he cancelled them when he heard we were goin' to church. *(He laughs into the air till laugh fades.)*

LILY. *(pause)* Were those men really looking at me?

CHARLES. Don't worry. *(pause)* TRUST me. *(She nods, pause. CHARLES looks in the direction where "those men" would be. Pause.)*

CHARLES. Do you want to sit closer? *(She nods. She moves her chair very close to his, staring at "those men." He puts his arm around the back of her chair. She looks at his arm there. He moves it. Pause.)*

LILY. My Aunt Ethel said she met your ex-wife once.

CHARLES. Yeah. I think she did. She was with the boyfriend at the time. Robert, I think his name was, the one she left for. *(pause)* Anaesthesiologist. He used to put her under and do her hair all *(Gestures.)* puffy, her makeup all *(Gestures)* WILD.

LILY. Wow.

CHARLES. He'd dress her all up to. Whatever he'd feel like at the time. She'd never know ahead of time. When she'd wake up, she'd look really wild. Totally new look. *(pause)* He could do that for her. I thought she looked fine the way she was, I — I really did, but — *(pause)*

LILY. Why did you stop being a doctor?

CHARLES. My eyesight.

LILY. What's wrong with your eyesight?

(She looks at his eyes. She sees something there. A tear. She shyly takes her finger to the corner of his eye. She removes hand. Charles doesn't look at her. She looks shyly away. MUSIC begins. A long pause, he drinks more of his drink, maybe finishes it. He smiles at her—)

CHARLES. You wanna dance? *(She nods. They dance. It is a slow one or sort of slow, so they do a sort of slow dance step. She keeps trying to lead and steps on his feet.)*

LILY. I'm not really good at this. I'm really bad at this.

CHARLES. No. You're O.K. Trust me. Just do what I do. Follow me. *(after a while—)* That's right. And relax.

LILY. *(a little while longer—)* Oh, God! I'm sorry. I'm clumsy.

CHARLES. It's O.K. Just let me lead. *(She nods. After a while, they are dancing close. After some time—)*

LILY. God, this is fun. This is kind of like in a movie from like the thirties or maybe forties. They knew how to dance then. My mother, who is old, the same as my aunt, her sister, who also has a daughter my age, Eloise, a change of life baby. Anyway, Oh yeah ... my mother and her sister were both — *(He stops her. They are close. He looks at her, something she was not able to do as she told her story.)* Sisters.

CHARLES. *(Smiles.)* You're doing it again. You're just talking because you're nervous.

LILY. No, I'm not. *(He looks at her. Pause. He walks to the table. She follows him awkwardly.)*

LILY. I'm sorry.

CHARLES. No, you're not.

LILY. Yes, I am.

CHARLES. O.K. Then what about?

LILY. That I made you mad.

CHARLES. About what?

LILY. I don't know. *(pause)* I don't really understand — *(pause, quietly—)* What about?

CHARLES. You use words for the wrong reason. You don't use them to communicate something to me. You just talk because you don't know what else to do and you're afraid.

LILY. NO, I'M NOT.

CHARLES. There you go again. Every time I try to get close to you—

LILY. I'm sorry.

CHARLES. "Sorry." What's sorry?

LILY. A word.

CHARLES. Words weren't made to be used that way. God didn't make words so we'd elude each other.

LILY. *(Smiles.)* God didn't make 'em to begin with.

CHARLES. He made them as a TOOL.

LILY. Like a hammer—

CHARLES. They are supposed to be a tool. They are supposed to *help* us *communicate. (He looks at her. Toward the end of his conversation she had been looking off to the side. He thinks she's not listening to him — he tells her this in a look.)*

LILY. I heard you. I heard everything you said. I swear to God. "God didn't make words so that we'd elude each other. He made them as a tool. They are supposed to *help* us to *communicate. (pause)* But I don't know what "elude" means, so some of it kind of, you lost me.

CHARLES. Elude, you know, to avoid, to escape. *(He looks at her. She looks at him. Pause.)*

CHARLES. Maybe we should just shut up before I say something bad and hurt you. Because I don't want to—

LILY. NO. You helped me. You taught me something. "Elude." And about *words* and *communication. (pause)* Maybe we should both shut up.

CHARLES. Really? Because I don't want to—

LILY. Really.

CHARLES. —hurt you. *(They look at each other. A pause.)*

LILY. Maybe if we didn't say anything.

CHARLES. Maybe if we just drank and didn't say anything.

(They laugh. The transition MUSIC begins. They sit up elegantly. They both lock the key and throw it away. They toast their new pact of silence with their real glasses from the prior scene. Then he shows her how to loop their arms so that she drinks from his glass and he from hers. He does a chaplinesque introduction of walking his fingers toward her and waving his hand. She is charmed and shyly does this to him. His two hands "dance" on the table. Then her hand and his hand dance together on the table. She has a idea. She takes out her notepad and writes something on it. He writes something back. They take the dance floor. They bow and curtsey and share an elegant happy dance until the MUSIC changes. When it does, he points to a clock. She goes to table, grabs sweater. She takes his hand and they run. They stop in the "church," make the sign of the cross, kneel and stick their tongues out for communion. When their tongues go back inside their mouths, they stand, he nods and takes her hand and they go back to the bar. He opens the door for her, orders two more drinks. They sit and wave to bartender silently, "MERRY CHRISTMAS." They again loop their arms so that they're feeding each other drinks. This time though they disentangle slowly, smile and look at each other. They come out of their position as MUSIC ends and a more tired and on-edge RICHARD and CICI Enter—)

RICHARD. How ya doin'? *(They nod.)* What you been up to? *(They shrug.)* Well like what? *(LILY writes something—)*

We haven't said anything in two hours? Why? *(CHARLES writes and he reads—)* We made a pact. *(He asks)* Why? *(They write and he reads—)* Because. *(CICI and RICHARD both ask—)* Because why?

RICHARD. *(of LILY and CHARLES who've just laughed)* Do they think we're stupid?

CICI. Honey go up there and buy 'em some more drinks. *(CHARLES and LILY gesture that they already have some.)* Well, we certainly need some more. Honey, go up there and get us some more. They won't come over and wait on us because it's Christmas and they're TOO DRUNK. *(She looks in her compact and puts make up on.)* What are you starin' at? Jesus! *(She puts make up on LILY.)* Move more toward me. I'd really like to get you in my chair. We do hair also. My boyfriend, Stephen, is a colorist. We could do blonde on you. And do it short. Something more modern. As it is now, you look very 60s, I don't know 60s, 70s. Maybe the Dark Ages or something. Your hair hanging like that. *(LILY looks at CHARLES.)*

LILY. Really? *(CHARLES shakes his head NO.)*

CICI. Certainly. Something shorter, lighter would lift you up like you wouldn't believe. Wouldn't it, honey?

RICHARD. You mean a little shirt or somethin'? *(Looks at LILY'S ... shirt.)*

CICI. No. Her HAIR.

RICHARD. Oh. Sure. *(pause)* So are they still deaf and dumb?

CICI. No. She's being sociable. This one — I don't know.

RICHARD. He's just drunk.

CHARLES. NO I'M NOT.

LILY. *(to CHARLES:)* It's O.K. We both are. It's fine. As long as you don't do it too often. You don't do you?

RICHARD. You want another one? *(CICI grabs his hand—)*

CICI. Listen, don't bother. Come back to our place. Really. It's tired here. Look around. Everyone is such a MESS. Let's LEAVE.

RICHARD. But I just got the drinks.

CICI. Take them with us. *(CICI stands, RICHARD fixes her skirt. RICHARD shyly smuggles his drink out. CICI does it out in the open — a display. They all leave the bar. They all leave and go to CICI'S and RICHARD'S motel room—)* It's not home, but it's like home. Show 'em, honey. *(He shows them his cocaine.)* Richard's real good at what he does, right, honey?

RICHARD. Right. *(pause, to CICI:)* Sit on my lap.

CICI. O.K. *(She sits there.)* The music was not *danceable* tonite of all nights. After a while it drives me crazy 'cause I don't know what they're sayin'.

RICHARD. Do you speak any Spanish?

LILY. No.

RICHARD. My grandparents are from Mexico. On my father's side. Anything you want to tell me, I tell you how to tell me.

LILY. O.K.

RICHARD. Es Verdad.

LILY. Es Verdad?

RICHARD. Is true.

LILY. That's kind of like O.K.

RICHARD. It *is* O.K.

LILY. All right.

RICHARD. I almost went to college, then the business got too good. The guy who's in with me, he went to college. History. I don't get it. FRANCE. *(Laughs.)* Phliosophy, psychology, something like that. That's a practical one. So you can figure it out, but it's too late now.

CICI. Richard almost went to college.

RICHARD. I'm telling them that. Weren't you here?

CICI. Oh.

RICHARD. Why don't you go change?

CICI. Should I go leopard?

RICHARD. Yeah, go leopard. *(She Exits.)* Isn't she something?

CHARLES. Yeah.

RICHARD. Well, isn't she?

CHARLES. She's really somethin'.

RICHARD. *(to CHARLES:)* You speak Spanish?

CHARLES. A little.

RICHARD. You don't, do you?

LILY. No.

RICHARD. Good. *(Pause, he tell him some personal thing about CICI in Spanish, some "guy" thing.)* You don't know what that means? *(CHARLES shakes his head.)* Wait till she comes out. She is so hot. We go to clubs and they can't keep their eyes off her. She's wild too. Ha? *(RICHARD smiles.)* She has no *fear.* Say we go to a club and I forget my I.D. and they want to see it, she breaks right past 'em, says a bunch of shit, grabs my hand and we're in! Don't you wish you looked like that?

LILY. Ah ha.

(CICI comes back out in a new outfit.)

RICHARD. Ha? What did I tell you? *(He adjusts her belt. She yells "Ow! Ow!.")* O.K.?

CICI. Yeah, it's O.K. *(She smiles to them an "It's O.K." smile.)* Honey, sit on the floor in front of me. I'm gonna rat your hair a little and they'll take a few pictures of us.

RICHARD. Chuckie, right?

CHARLES. Charles.

RICHARD. What do you do for a living?

CHARLES. Tile.

RICHARD. Tile?

CHARLES. I lay tile.

LILY. He used to be a doctor but he quit because his eyesight got too bad.

RICHARD. You need good eyes to lay tile too.

LILY. You do?

RICHARD. Sure.

CICI. Your eyes look O.K. to me.

CHARLES. Do you have any water?

CICI. Sure. *(Points to "other room" Exit stage left. CHARLES Exits.)*

LILY. He has a picture of him and his ex-wife next to a giant liver. He has his gloves on and a doctor coat and everything. His wife is looking at him as if she came right out of his rib. She adored him, it looks like and he *(pause)* loves her so much...

CICI. Bet he has a gentle bedside manner.

LILY. I wouldn't know. *(pause)* I bet though, too. *(He Enters.)* Are you O.K.?

CHARLES. Fine. *(After a long pause, LILY looks at CHARLES, gestures "lock the key and throw it away." As she's throwing it, he grabs her hand, smiles and shakes his head.)*

RICHARD. Wanna see what I can do?

LILY. Sure.

RICHARD. Sit down, Cici.

CICI. Honey!

RICHARD. Com'on.

CICI. You're too drunk.

RICHARD. Do it.

CICI. Wait till the wedding pictures. We told 'em we were gonna get married after breakfast—

RICHARD. Before. *(He does her hair and fucks it all up. She looks in mirror and laughs hysterically. CHARLES and LILY laugh too.)* It's not funny. What are you laughing at?

CICI. Oh Richard, it's hysterical.

RICHARD. No, it's not. I DID IT. It's not hysterical. Stop laughing. STOP — *(RICHARD almost hits CICI. They all stop laughing.)* It's the way I like it.

CICI. Stephen is the only one who can do it right. You know that.

RICHARD. Stephen! *(RICHARD runs behind screen. CICI follows—)*

CICI. Hey, don't rip anything up. Don't destroy any of my beauty supplies. DON'T SPRAY THAT AT ME! *(RICHARD chases CICI back into the room with a container of hair spray. He pins her to a wall. He puts the hair spray way above his head, away from her. She tries to get it—)* Com'on. Please. Please. PLEASE.

RICHARD. PL-EASE. *(pause)* STOP WHINING. *(She does, pause.)* Stop hanging on me. *(She does, pause.)* Stop being so pushy. *(They stare at one another. She grabs for the can. He keeps it from her.)*

Cici. *(pause)* He's jealous cause all my nice boyfriends are gay and he's not, so he doesn't know how to do hair. They're responsible for my look and he's not. He'd like to be responsible for it, too.

Richard. Who buys you the shit?

Cici. You. Who picks it out?

Richard. ME!   Cici. STEPHEN!

Richard. *(to CHARLES:)* We gotta get outta here. *(ready to leave)*

Cici. Where you goin'?

Richard. To get some beers.

Cici. To get some beers? *(as he's leaving—)* TAKE A PICTIRE. *(RICHARD comes back into the room. CICI hands the camera to CHARLES. She frantically holds onto RICHARD and smiles for the camera. RICHARD smiles too, but the second after the picture is taken, he storms out of the room. CHARLES gives CICI the camera, waves "Bye" to LILY and follows after RICHARD. CICI watches them leave. Pause. CICI lights a cigarette.)* Stephen is the best stylist. Stephen loves me *so* much. He gives me the way I look. Before I met him, I was in between boyfriends, after little Jacques was born, I was like you, sort of, look-wise. Now look at me.

(CICI smiles, then looks away from LILY. Her smile fades. LILY looks at her. She catches LILY looking at her. LILY looks away. A Mexican Christmas SONG begins playing in the motel room next door.)

Lily. I read in the paper that Tammy Fay Bakker, that

religious guy's wife, that she sleeps with eyelashes on. She cried on Ted Koppel and it was like her whole face fell onto her cheek and flooded down it like a rippling stream.

CICI. She doesn't use good mascara.

LILY. She's very afraid for him to see her like she is. You know, without, just regular. She has a hairdresser and all he has to do, his whole life is her hair.

CICI. Really?

LILY. I think so.

(Pause. The MUSIC in the next motel room becomes much louder.)

CICI. Time for me to freshen up my cocktail. *(CICI goes behind screen. She comes back with a pair of black sexy boots.)* Do you like these boots?

LILY. I love them.

CICI. He is gonna flip. I wish they'd stop playing this music. *I DON'T UNDERSTAND WHAT THEY'RE SAY-ING!! (She angrily throws boots at the wall upstage where the music is coming from in the room next door. A beat after the boots hits the wall, the MUSIC stops. CICI smiles with satisfaction and is instantly calm. She sits and asks LILY—)* You don't go to clubs?

LILY. No.

CICI. What do you do for fun?

LILY. Go to the movies. And rent old ones. My mother's really old 'cause I was a change of life baby along with my cousin, Eloise. I was named after Lillian Gish. *(Smiles.)* Mostly I like tap dance ones and ones with lots of tears and romance. On ships.

Cici. Oh sure. Like "The Love Boat." That "genre."

Lily. Oh no—

Cici. Like other "themes." "Deeper" themes.

Lily. Right.

Cici. You haven't had a date in a while?

Lily. No, but—

Cici. But months?

Lily. Yeah, but—

Cici. But you don't mind?

Lily. No, I mind, but — *(LILY looks away. CICI looks at her. She catches CICI looking at her. CICI looks away. Pause.)*

Cici. Wanna see my wallet while I do your hair? *(She takes out her wallet and begins clipping some of LILY'S long hair up on her head with hair clips. LILY looks at CICI'S pictures.)*

Lily. Oh, you look very muscular like a jock there.

Cici. Yeah, that's when Johnny and me was into that.

Lily. Who's that on the Harley?

Cici. That's me. And that's me recently, but not NOW. My looks, ha? Like a chameleon. That's why I choose my line of work.

Lily. It's all about beauty?

Cici. Hell, no. It's all about FASHION. Fashion can be UG-ly. But sometimes they go together. That's always nice! *(touching her own hair—)* He did it way too conservative. *(pause)* O.K. now. Which is better: a heroine addict or an alcoholic?

TAKE A PICTURE

LILY. I — I don't know, which?

CICI. *(Laughs.)* I don't know. *(serious—)* Sometimes I wish I did. He's very much in love with me, you can tell that, ha?

LILY. Sure.

CICI. It's just sometimes, he's stoned and it makes him kinda nasty, but then I'M stoned and I get horny. And sometimes we're not on the same thing — Yeah, it's a problem. We gotta find the "appropriate" combination of drugs for us both to be on at the same time so we'll be in the same mood at the same time, then we'll be home free — Nothing's wrong with us, it's just our shit's a little contradictory—

LILY. Well—

CICI. You seem to think differently. What do you think?

LILY. Well — I don't know.

CICI. Go ahead. You thought something. I could see you think it—

LILY. Well — *(pause)* It's like he was saying something and then you were saying something, but you didn't listen to him and he didn't listen to you—

CICI. Oh, that's all — *(Smiles.)* We do that all the time. We don't say anything worth listening to anyway. You don't have to hear what someone says to love them. That's for sure. *(Her smile fades when she realizes the thought. CICI looks away. LILY looks at her. She catches LILY looking at her. LILY looks away. Pause.)* Honey, you have to pay attention to your womanhood more, really. Let me show you a few things. Rip off those little socks. Go ahead. Do now. *(LILY does.)* Good. Let me see. *(Finds stockings behind screen—)* Try these on. I got them originally at Robinson's, I think. At the Santa Monica Mall.

LILY. I haven't been there.

CICI. That's right. You're new. *(of stockings—)* Go ahead, don't be shy. You get 'em dirty, we'll just wash 'em out and hang 'em on the patio. Look at the patio. Yeah, that's why we chose this hotel over all the others. The nice patio views. Don't be shy. *(LILY smiles.)* You have nice legs. No, you do. Really.

LILY. Thank you.

CICI. You don't like sexy things, ha?

LILY. No. I mean—

CICI. Yeah, I heard that. Someone told me that about the East Coast. That they don't like sexy things. They're way conservative. And kind of stuck up. You know, polyester. Am I right? *(pause)* Oh, I'm sorry. I don't mean it relating to you. Just trends. You need a garter to go with it. *(She gets garter and Tecate*.)* You know I'm really into fashion, I love it very much. You really do have nice legs. *(instantly loud—)* WHERE THE HELL ARE THEY? *(Throws beer can.)*

LILY. I don't know.

CICI. *(instantly calm—)* O.K. Then, here's my garter. You can go in there and put it on if you're embarrassed me watching you — *(LILY goes into "other room." Loud so LILY can hear her—)* WHEN I WORKED OUT AT THE GYM — when me and Johnny, my boyfriend and ex-lover in 1979, when we belonged to the Sports Connection, I noticed some girls shy like you, they would never

*Tecate: Mexican brand beer.

take a shower. They wouldn't smell badly or any— *(LILY Enters.)* Oh you're done. Good. O.K. Take off your shirt.

LILY. Why?

CICI. We're gonna put you in a little camisole to flatter your figure — you have a nice chest, you know that, don't you?

LILY. I don't know.

CICI. I noticed Richard admiring it. He told me he thought highly of it. O.K. You can go in the other room. *(LILY goes, to change.)* I DON'T KNOW WHERE THEY FUCKIN' ARE — IF RICHARD GOES TO JAIL AGAIN, THEY'RE GONNA HASSLE ME. THEY'RE GONNA HASSLE ME AND GIVE ME SHIT THAT I DON'T NEED. He's such a fucking ASShole when he's fucked up. *(LILY Enters in a very feminine but VERY little camisole. She is shy. CICI is instantly calm—)* Oh, yeah, that's lovely. It's too big on me, obviously. You care for another cocktail, honey?

LILY. Well—

CICI. Listen — I'll dump that one out. It's loose with all the ice shining and melting in there. I'll give you a new cocktail. *(CICI comes back without drinks—)* Do you wanna see my tattoo? *(Unbuttons shirt, shows LILY her upper arm—)* I got it when I wasn't really thinking. Topper, the guy on the motorcycle in that picture — he told me to get it. And so I did. Do you do things when people tell you to?

LILY. Sometimes.

CICI. *(quietly—)* After we broke up, I tried getting rid of it. Make-up. And I almost burned it. Someone told me you light a match to it and it disintegrates, but they were fucked up when they told me that, I realized it just in time. *(Looks at her.)* Would you kiss it? *(CICI looks away from her—)* Please? *(pause)* Ha? *(pause)* It'll never go away. *(CICI sits on LILY'S lap and holds her.)* I'm scared ... I — I don't know what to do. Don't tell anyone promise? ... Hold me tight. My sister used to hold me tight like this when we were little but she ran off with an organ grinder, this guy with a monkey she met in the park when she was tryin' to buy me some dope. And she's in Michigan with two kids now. She's very, very, very fat. She didn't used to be. She's afraid to go outside. So she stays in lots and now she's afraid to go out 'cause someone'll see her. She's afraid of herself FAT like that. She's afraid of herself. *(pause)* Give me a tight one. Please. *(LILY holds her tight.)* I love you very much. *(pause)* Oh wait a second, I'll get us a treat. There's some left.

LILY. *(of a pot pipe CICI'S brought out from behind screen—)* No, thanks, I don't remember myself when I do that and it makes me—

CICI. I don't remember myself either, and I like it. I don't remember myself *and* I don't understand myself. That happens *all* the time, though. *(Smiles till smile fades.)* Oh, I'll get you some shoes to complete the look. I'll have to take you shopping. You don't wear high heals very often?

LILY. Oh, no. I get these awful bunions.

CICI. PL-*EASE.*

(LILY sits with the camisole, nylons, long skirt on. Some of her hair is clipped on the top of her head. She is bending over to examine her foot, crossing one leg over the other. CICI is standing to the side of

her. She doesn't have her shirt on, but she wears a black bra. She looks at LILY. The men come in. LILY shyly holds the camisole to her. CICI just stands there with her cigarette and waves "hi." LILY says excuse me and leaves for the other room to put more on. Before she leaves, RICHARD looks at her a certain way.)

RICHARD. She's a nice girl.

CICI. She is. She's very nice. Was showin' her my tattoo.

RICHARD. I told you to cover that thing up. *(RICHARD walks around the room, CICI follows him—)*

CICI. I can't help it. You can't get rid of it. Told you that. How many times?

RICHARD. Don't show him.

CICI. I won't. I'm sorry.

RICHARD. *(Mocks her—)* "I'm sorry." What's sorry? So what?

CICI. Cover me up then — Please, please, please.

RICHARD. *(Mocks her—)* Please, please, please — *(He teases her by holding her shirt way above his head. She tries to reach it and can't. Finally he gently puts her arms in the shirt and buttons it up. They kiss. Pause.)* Can't you stop whining?

CICI. I'm trying to remember.

RICHARD. Maybe you should shut up.

CICI. Only if you do.

RICHARD. I have things to say.

CICI. So do I.

RICHARD. Like what?

CICI. Don't push it. It's Christmas.

RICHARD. *(Mocks her—)* "It's Christmas." *(CICI has her cocktail glass way above her head. CHARLES grabs it from her and gently puts it down.)*

CHARLES. You want to touch it up?

CICI. Surely. *(CICI smiles at CHARLES as he freshens up his drink and her drink with the vodka he just bought. CHARLES sees this and—)*

RICHARD. O.K. Now's good. *(to CHARLES:)* Take a picture. Her and me, on the patio. *(He smiles.)* Well no. Wait a second. Kiss me. No don't kiss me like that. Wait a second. Kind of sexier. Let's see. I'll like, you know, bend you over like in one of those Cary Grant movies. You look swept off your feet. We'll send it to your sister in Michigan. What's her name?

CICI. Stacey.

RICHARD. Stacey.

(LILY re-enters.)

LILY. Oh great. That looks like an old Cary Grant movie. *(regarding RICHARD'S and CICI'S pose)*

RICHARD. You think so?

LILY. Sure.

RICHARD. That's what I was goin' for. *(to CHARLES:)* Hold on. *(to LILY:)* You wanna be in it?

LILY. Well—

RICHARD. No. Com'on. We've got plenty of the two of us together. You and me. *(LILY shyly takes CICI'S place for the picture. RICHARD bends her over in that pose and actually kisses her. LILY looks at CHARLES when she's done.)*

CICI. *(to CHARLES:)* Freshen it up a little more, ha? You want some more, Lillian?

LILY. Lily. *(pause)* No, thanks.

TAKE A PICTURE 39

Cici. Maybe one of me and him — *(of CHARLES)* You know like "Last Tango in Paris!" *(CICI goes to kiss him. CHARLES and CICI kiss. CICI backs away from him.)* I was only jokin'. *(She laughs.)*

Richard. You're not very funny.

Cici. PL-*EASE*. Just because you can't take a joke — *(RICHARD and CICI stare at each other. Then they look at LILY and CHARLES. They smile to LILY and CHARLES, "It's O.K." They kiss.)* It's our wedding day, honey. Can I have some Christmas snow, please?

(Our final transition scene begins. As the MUSIC starts, they all sit up properly. Then CICI and RICHARD snort cocaine. CHARLES has his turn. LILY tries to but almost sneezes it all out. They all lean toward her, but she doesn't sneeze after all. MUSIC changes and they dance a very happy, very hyper dance: first, the two couples; then, the men dance together and the women dance together. After the playful dance, MUSIC changes again. RICHARD takes out his wallet full of pictures. They all sit and show pictures. RICHARD shows one of his old girlfriend. "She makes my heart flutter," he gestures. "She's too fat," CICI explains to LILY and CHARLES in a gesture. Then, CICI shows a picture of her old boyfriend. She bites her knuckles, he's so cute. RICHARD points to his head and gestures, "He has no brains." CICI asks to see a picture from LILY. When CICI sees, she turns her foot out. To explain, LILY demonstrates how her mother walks before and after the foot gear and CICI follows behind her to try and copy her so that she can understand the walk. They sit. CICI asks to see CHARLES' picture. He gestures, "No." She gestures, "Please." When CICI sees the picture, she asks him, "Is that a heart?" He shows her, "No. A liver." CICI tells CHARLES, "She's beautiful."

He smiles and nods. After a beat, she gestures by pulling an imaginary ring off her finger and throwing it, referring to his wife leaving him. She laughs aloud. RICHARD and LILY laugh aloud too. LILY realizes what she's laughing at and stops. RICHARD realizes it and also stops. CICI keeps laughing. MUSIC ends as CHARLES' smile fades as he stares at picture. RICHARD nudges CICI and she stops laughing. She doesn't understand why everyone's become so quiet—)

CICI. *(to RICHARD:)* What's wrong?

RICHARD. Nothing.

CICI. You know, we're all dressed up except him. How would you like to see him?

LILY. I like him the way he is.

CICI. Yeah, but wouldn't you like to see him modern? I'll get something of Richard's. *(CICI takes the shirt off RICHARD'S back. He watches in disbelief.)* Put it on him. *(to LILY:)* You don't mind, do you? *(CHARLES shakes his head. LILY reluctantly does as CICI says.)* OK. Take his shirt off. *(pause)* He'll go along with it, won't you? Do with him as you will. Do it. Rat his hair. Do it. People like to be told what to do. Especially when they're tired.

CICI. Please, PLEASE, let me just see what he looks like. *(to CHARLES:)* You look so much better modern. You really do. God! I betcha that has something to do with why your wife left you, because you stayed the same way—

LILY. *(after a pause)* Let's dance. *(LILY and CHARLES dance slowly and tightly. CICI stares at them. Pause.)*

CICI. Take a picture. Take a picture. Take a PICture. Please. Please—

RICHARD. Shut up. SHUT up. Cici, Cici, look. Look what you did. Sh! *(CICI is insistent. She grabs for him. She grabs for his camera. She whines.)*

CICI. What I did.

RICHARD. Sh! Please. Please. Be quiet now. BE QUIET NOW. Cici? Cici? I'm gonna have to keep you away from them. Leave them alone. Don't. I'm warning you — Cici! *(He slaps her across the face. She falls on the bed. She is quiet. She quietly sits on the bed. He follows her. He puts her face in his lap—)* I'm so sorry.

CICI. Sorry? What's sorry?

RICHARD. You... you talk without thinking. You "hurt" his feelings. You ... You didn't mean to. You just talk because ... you're afraid.

CICI. NO I'M NOT.

RICHARD. And so you talk. And I don't hear you and you don't hear me. *(pause)* I'm sorry. I'm *really* sorry — I'm — *(She covers his mouth. She gestures, "Wait." She brings back some tape. They tape each other's mouths shut. Then they just hold each other like two frightened children. CHARLES and LILY see this. They know it's time to leave. They look at each other, take off all their RICHARD and CICI clothing and fold it neatly on a chair. Then—)*

LILY. Guess we'll be seeing you. *(CHARLES gestures "Bye." LIGHTS stay on the taped couple. Up on LILY and CHARLES in the bar. He's about to say something, opens mouth, closes it. She's about to say something, opens mouth, closes it. They look back toward where CICI and RICHARD are. They look at each other. Nervously, she begins to say, "I — " They keep looking at each other. She closes her mouth. The LIGHTS fade as their lips come together in a kiss—)*

THE END

MUSIC

During the original production of the play, three kinds of Mexican music were used. A wonderful tape of quirky instrumental music, waltzes reminiscent of something that might underscore a silent movie, played underneath our silent movies: the transitions. Each transition should last two to three minutes and each should tell a story and suggest passing of time. The transitions occur on pages 12, 24, & 39. The sane "theme" music that helps tell our story during the transitions should help set the mood for our tale as well. In addition to the three songs used during transitions, two more songs from this same tape should be used: one to begin the play, the other immediately after the play ends. A fast-moving, but passionate and highly romantic song should underscore the action from the moment Lily follows Charles out of the motel room the second time and should continue through Richard's and Cici's initial entrance. That song should fade out as Richard and Cici join Lily and Charles. The song should come up very loudly immediately after Lily says, "NO I'M NOT." It should, in a sense, be Richard's and Cici's theme song, preparing us for the drama of their romance. The transition music is, in a sense, Lily's and Charles' theme song. The two dance songs in the bar scenes should be old-fashioned in a sense, as music is very important in creating the quirky world of this play.

PERSONAL PROPS AND COSTUME

LILY—

In purse:
> pen, paper, electrology card, picture of mom, wallet

In suitcase:
> clothes, bag with panties and bras, shoes

Costume:
> green shirt, green skirt, black sweater, socks, practi cal little shoes, glasses

CHARLES—

In pockets:
> wallet with pictures of him and wife, "grass," small bottle of tequila, cigarettes and matches

In suitcase:
> clothes

Carrying:
> water jug and jacket to suit coat

Costume:
> white shirt, old-fashioned tie, green suit (jackets and pants) that was once nice, but is now out-of-date and old-fashioned, glasses

44   TAKE A PICTURE

RICHARD—
In pockets:
>   wallet with picture of old girlfriend

Carrying:
>   camera (preferably Polaroid with film)

Costume:
>   shirt and pants and shoes which look "modern"

CICI—
In purse:
>   clip for Lily's hair, comb, brush, cigarettes and matches, wallet with pictures of old beaus and Jacques, compact with mirror

Costume:
>   very modern, perhaps— tight black spandex pants, sexy, but feminine little shirt with off-the-shoulder sleeves, high heels

Costume:
>   (set behind screen or backstage left, if there is a backstage left) similar to original costume, but with a leopard pattern/motif

FURNITURE PRE-SET

In Bar—
>Two matching chairs USR
>Two matching chairs (same as those USR) and one small round table DSR

In Motel—
>One full or queen-size bed against USL wall
>One dressing screen R of bed
>Two chairs that don't match in front of dressing screen
>One small stool (optional) behind dressing screen to hold props

PROP PRE-SET

Behind dressing screen—
Camisole, nylons and garter belt
Big ashtray
Black boots
Can of hairspray
Pot pipe
Can of Tecate or other brand of beer (preferably Mexican)
Nail polish or other cosmetics which Richard rummages through during fight
One glass with margarita in it

Underwear which Cici rummages through and throws on bed while looking for clothes for Lily
Tape

Backstage—
Eight to ten margarita glasses filled with margarita-looking drink
Six-pack of Tecate (or other, preferably Mexican beer) which men bring when they return

In Bar—
Green tablecloth and ashtray on table

In Motel—
Cocaine mirror and "cocaine" in baggie under bed
Bedspread on bed with two pillows beneath it

CHAIR

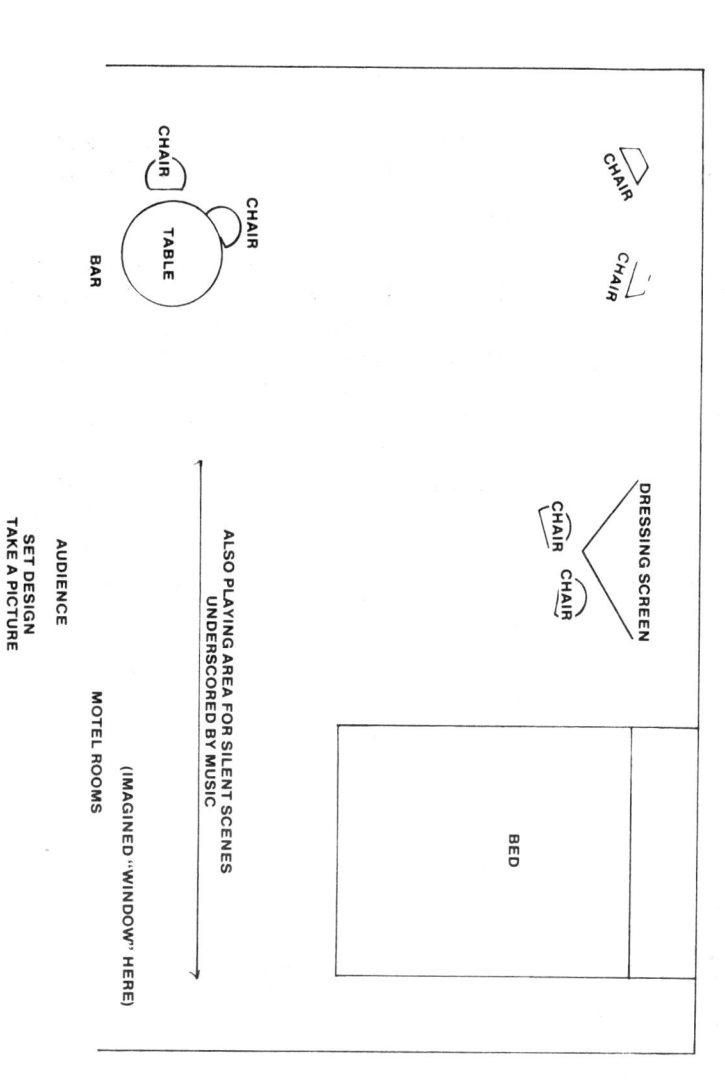

CHAIR

TABLE

BAR

CHAIR

CHAIR

DRESSING SCREEN

CHAIR

CHAIR

ALSO PLAYING AREA FOR SILENT SCENES
UNDERSCORED BY MUSIC

BED

AUDIENCE

**SET DESIGN
TAKE A PICTURE**

MOTEL ROOMS

(IMAGINED "WINDOW" HERE)

Other Publications for Your Interest

THE CURATE SHAKESPEARE AS YOU LIKE IT
(LITTLE THEATRE—COMEDY)
By DON NIGRO

4 men, 3 women—Bare stage

This extremely unusual and original piece is subtitled: "The record of one company's attempt to perform the play by William Shakespeare". When the very prolific Mr. Nigro was asked by a professional theatre company to adapt *As You Like It* so that it could be performed by a company of seven he, of course, came up with a completely original play about a rag-tag group of players comprised of only seven actors led by a dotty old curate who nonetheless must present Shakespeare's play; and the dramatic interest, as well as the comedy, is in their hilarious attempts to impersonate all of Shakespeare's multitude of characters. The play has had numerous productions nationwide, all of which have come about through word of mouth. We are very pleased to make this "underground comic classic" widely available to theatre groups who like their comedy wide open and theatrical. (#5742)

(Royalty, $50-$25.)

SEASCAPE WITH SHARKS AND DANCER
(LITTLE THEATRE—DRAMA)
By DON NIGRO

1 man, 1 woman—Interior

This is a fine new play by an author of great talent and promise. We are very glad to be introducing Mr. Nigro's work to a wide audience with *Seascape With Sharks and Dancer*, which comes directly from a sold-out, critically acclaimed production at the world-famous Oregon Shakespeare Festival. The play is set in a beach bungalow. The young man who lives there has pulled a lost young woman from the ocean. Soon, she finds herself trapped in his life and torn between her need to come to rest somewhere and her certainty that all human relationships turn eventually into nightmares. The struggle between his tolerant and gently ironic approach to life and her strategy of suspicion and attack becomes a kind of war about love and creation which neither can afford to lose. In other words, this is quite an offbeat, wonderful love story. We would like to point out that the play also contains a wealth of excellent **monologue** and **scene material.** (#21060)

(Royalty, $50-$35.)